I0481547

Network Marketing

*The Complete Guide On How to Create a
Profitable Network Marketing Business
Using Online Strategies and Techniques*

*(Learn Proven Online and Social Media Techniques
That Will Propel Your Business to the Next Level)*

Anthony James

The information in the following pages is broadly considered to be a truthful and accurate account of facts, and as such any inattention, use or misuse of the information in question by the reader will render any resulting actions solely under their purview. There are no scenarios in which the publisher or the original author of this work can be in any fashion deemed liable for any hardship or damages that may befall them after undertaking information described herein.

Additionally, the information found on the following pages is intended for informational purposes only and should thus be considered, universal. As befitting its nature, the information presented is without assurance regarding its continued validity or interim quality. Trademarks that mentioned are done without written consent and can in no way be considered an endorsement from the trademark holder.

Contents

Introduction

Thank you for purchasing *Network Marketing: The Complete Guide On How to Create a Profitable Network Marketing Business Using Online Strategies and Techniques (Learn Proven Online and Social Media Techniques That Will Propel Your Business to the Next Level).*

This book is dedicated to helping you begin your own thriving network marketing business in a way that will ensure you are massively successful. With the tips and tricks provided in this book, you will be able to rapidly progress in your company and eventually become a top-level earner. This book is created for those who are truly dedicated to generating massive success in their business and in their teams. If this sounds like you, then you are in the right place.

Unlike other books that promote tacky and desperate strategies, this book will teach you to become a natural-born business leader. Because, my friend, you are running a real business and it deserves to be organized that way. You are not going to learn about the ineffective and often embarrassing strategies that are being promoted in the uneducated network marketing community. Instead, you are going to learn to be a charismatic leader who attracts leads effortlessly.

Throughout each chapter, you are going to learn about a unique part of your business that is important to your success. You will learn how to build a solid foundation through effective brand-building strategies, which will enable you to have the best opportunity to launch your successful network marketing business.

Then, you will learn about effective lead-generating strategies that will literally bring clients to you. Instead of having to chase people down and encourage them to join your business or buy your products, they will be begging you to join! This is one of the best parts of being a network marketing business *leader*. You stay clear of being held back by the "employee" mindset and you take on the "leadership" role, which truly has a profound impact on your business. This book will teach you exactly how to do that.

Additionally, you are going to learn about how to effectively sell your products and grow your business. In essence, you are going to learn about everything you need to know in order to have success with your business. This book will teach you how you can start from the ground up, and maintain and grow your business to top-level income earning success. If you are ready to become a leader and generate massive success in your network marketing business, then you are ready to read *Network Marketing: The Complete Guide On How to Create a Profitable Network Marketing Business Using Online Strategies and Techniques (Learn Proven Online and Social Media Techniques That Will Propel Your Business to the Next Level).*

Chapter 1: Choosing Your Company

The very first step in building a successful network marketing company, before anything else, is choosing exactly what company you want to be a part of. There are so many different companies that are available in a variety of unique niches, which can make this process slightly difficult. Which company you will choose to represent will rely heavily on your interests, however, there are many other things that you need to consider as well.

It can be easy to want to jump into a business simply because you see your friends doing it, but this isn't always the best reason to join. Since you are committing to a business, you want to make sure that you are partnering with a company that is going to give you the best opportunity to create massive success. There are many things to consider and this chapter is going to explore exactly what you need to think about when you are choosing what network marketing company you want to represent your business.

If you have already dedicated yourself to a business that you love, it is worthwhile to complete this section anyway. While you will not be undergoing the process of committing to a new business, it can help to know the answers to the questions that will be explored here. Knowing these answers will help you encourage potential new team members to understand the value of your company, and why it is such a positive company to partner with.

If you are already with a company but you are unsure as to whether you want to stay, then it is especially important that you pay attention to this section. You want to make sure that you are partnering with a company that is going to help you with your success. Even though you may have already invested funds and time into building your business, if you find that you are not one hundred percent happy with your choice, you may want to choose a new business. A very large part of your success is reliant on you being completely happy with your business so that you can passionately promote it and share it with others. If you cannot confidently do this, you may not have much success with your business.

Pick Something That Interests You

The very first part of choosing your new network marketing company is to consider what categories actually interest you. There are many people who are quick to jump into a network marketing company because they see others succeeding with it and they get swindled by a promise to "get rich quick". When they do this, they don't always take the time to consider whether or not they are actually interested in the business they have partnered with. Just because an opportunity is worthwhile for someone else does not mean it is worthwhile for you. You want to choose a company that accurately reflects you and your unique interests and passions.

Being successful in network marketing starts with having a personal passion for the company you are selling for. While it doesn't have to be your number one passion, it should be something that relates directly to your number one passion. This makes it easier for you to actually sell the products since you believe in them. When you don't believe in the products or services, you will struggle to sell them as people will see through your sales pitches and sense the lack of passion you have for the products. People who are passionate about what they sell are usually naturals at selling it.

When you are picking something that interests you, consider your lifestyle. What type of company would fit in well with your lifestyle? What is something that people already know you love? You want to pick a company that is going to reflect this about you. This way, it makes sense why you joined, and people can genuinely believe that you are passionate about the products and services and that you truly believe in them.

If you have many interests and passions, like most people do, try and stick to the one that will be most sustainable for you. Pick one that you are going to enjoy talking about and sharing for a long time. You want to build a business that is sustainable, so completing this step is important.

Look at The Company's Story

Every company has a story and knowing your potential company's story is important. When you are considering a company, you want to take the time to pay attention to this story. This story will help you see if you relate to the company. It usually shares the brand message and gives you a feel for what the company is all about. You want to pick a company with a story that inspires you and makes you feel passionate about the company and what they are aspiring to accomplish with their business.

Having a personal passion for the story and goal of a company will help you feel more personally connected to the business. Remember, this is going to be *your* business, so you want it to align with you as much as it possibly can. The more you feel personally connected to and inspired by the company, the more it will feel as though it is your own. This will make it easier for you to own your position in business and market yourself as the expert in your company. It will help you immensely when it comes to growing your sales and building a team, so make sure you take the time to pay attention to this part of the story.

Consider the Current Growth Rate of the Company

Many companies share information about their growth rates online. However, they will often accentuate their greatest period of growth. Take some time to do some research and look into their recent growth rates. This will give you the opportunity to see exactly what their growth is like right now, which is important. Many network marketing companies experience rapid growth for the first few years in business, then they plateau and slowly lose numbers in sales and growth. The exact lifespan of each company varies, but they can be learned through watching the numbers.

Learn the Commission Structure

Knowing the commission structure of the company you are considering is important. Every company has a different commission structure, so you want to pay attention to how this works. You can generally find the commission structure on each company's website under the "join" section.

When you are looking at the commission structure, look for two things: how you get paid at each level, and what it takes for you to get to each level. Some companies make it easier for you to get to the next level than others. Some also pay more than others. It is important to understand where your income is coming from and how, as this will help you have success with the business.

Research the Company's Brand and Reputation

Most of the information you learned up until now could be found on the company's website, but now you want to close out of that and research them elsewhere. Do some research on the company to see what their reputation is like and what people think of the brand.

Remember, there are many skeptics out there so you will find a lot of negative reviews virtually on every network marketing company. Believe it or not, many times these come from people who are a part of a different company and want to tarnish the reviews of other companies to encourage their followers to join them. Instead of looking at each individual review, take them all and look at the average message you read with each.

What you really want to know is how their brand is perceived by people. Some brands are known for offering faulty products that simply aren't worth purchasing. You don't want to be part of a brand like this. Other brands are associated with scandals that give the entire company and brand a bad name, and you don't want to be associated with anything like that. Try and find yourself a brand that is positive and that people like to represent and purchase from. This will make it easier when it comes to growing your business because you will not be swimming upstream with having your leads being drawn away by a bad business reputation that is beyond your control.

Ask Other People Who Have Been with That Company

Taking the time to ask other people who have been with the company about how their experience is or was is important. You should speak with your potential upline, but also speak with others as well. Ask people who are at all levels of the commission scale, and those who are no longer with the company, and ask what their experience is or was. How did they feel about their ability to generate growth within' the business? Were they able to create success? Did they feel as though their specific upline helped them along the way? Did they feel supported? Did they get provided with all of the information and resources required to run a successful business? Knowing information like this is important when it comes to establishing and running your own network marketing company. Again, take the time to listen to these people's average message and don't get heavily invested in any specific person. Some people have a higher drive to succeed than others, so you never know exactly what went into formulating each opinion. However, when you look at the average message you can get an idea of what the company will actually be like.

Choosing Your Upline

Before you commit to any single company, choose your upline carefully. You want to choose an upline that is having success with their business, and that will be able to help you have success with yours. Pay attention to their team, what they are doing to help their team, and how committed they are.

Any upline is going to seem dedicated to your success entirely when they are wanting to recruit you. However, only some will remain passionate about your success on an ongoing basis. Most companies have dedicated leaders who are committed to helping their teams succeed. These are people who are doing regular team-building activities, hosting webinars to help you succeed, and are invested in supporting their team. You want someone like this, not someone who is going to retreat and leave you to your own devices as soon as you have signed up. You can learn about this information by asking other members of their team.

Making Your Decision

Once you have taken the time to research each company, you are ready to make your decision! By now, you should have all of the information you need to make an informed decision.

When it comes to committing to a company, you want to take a look at all of the facts you have learned about each company. Then, you want to pay attention to how you actually feel about each company. You most likely have established some preferences towards certain companies over others. This feeling is important, as you want to feel strongly about the company you choose to join.

In addition to choosing a company you feel good about, you want to choose one that is going to give you as many resources as possible to help you succeed. While it is up to you to put the work in and go for it, you want to make sure that you are choosing a company that is going to support you as much as possible in your success.

Chapter 2: Establishing Your Brand

Once you have chosen the company you are going to work with, you want to establish your brand. Just because the company itself has a brand doesn't mean you can't (or shouldn't) have your own unique brand that you'll use to identify your unique business. This chapter is going to explain the importance of your branding and help you establish a brand that will set you apart from the company as a whole.

Why You Need to Establish Your Brand

Establishing your brand will have many incredible benefits for your business. It is important that you establish your brand before you begin sharing and marketing your business.

When you establish a brand, you can set yourself apart from other marketers in your company. It makes you look like an expert who is extremely passionate about the business, which means that people will be more likely to look for your help instead of looking elsewhere.

When you uniquely brand your business personally, people will connect with your personal story and message and want to do business with you, instead of someone else who may be doing business under generic company branding.

One additional benefit you get from branding your business is that you can share the brand with your team. This way, your unique brand will continue to grow as your team does. It reflects very positively on you and gives your new team members the benefit of knowing exactly what brand they should be reflecting in their own business.

It is absolutely imperative that you choose a brand and stick with it when you are building your own network marketing business. Remember, you are a real business marketer, and you need to act like one if you are going to have real success! Part of that is establishing a powerful brand that you will be able to share with your leads and use to set your business apart from the company overall.

What You Need to Ask Yourself When Branding

There are many things you need to consider when you are in the process of building a brand for your business. Your brand will be your entire image and message, so you need to be certain that you pick one that is personal to you and that will relate to people as well.

When you are building your brand, there are several questions you should ask yourself. The first being "Why did I choose *this* company?" The answer to this specific question is going to give you a lot of information that you need when you are building your company. First, it is going to help you identify what your overall message is. For example, if you chose a health-based company because you wanted to dedicate to your health more, then your message will be that the company is a pivoting point for those who want to take control over their health. This message will also help you determine your target audience. For your unique business, you will be targeting people who want to be healthier in their lives.

To contrast how your message affects your brand, let's imagine you answer the question differently. Perhaps you joined the company because you are passionate about your health and you were seeking for a new product to enjoy as a part of your healthy routine. In this case, your message is that your brand is an expert in healthy products and routines, and you are targeting people who are already a part of the health industry. You are not targeting those who are ready to start taking responsibility for your health, you are now targeting those who already have.

Generally, you want to target people who are in a similar position as you are, or were when you started your business. This will make your message extremely personal and will help people feel connected to you and your brand.

Another question you want to ask yourself is how you want your target audience to feel. This will help you determine exactly how you want to position yourself so that you can speak directly to your audience.

Elements of Your Brand That Are Important

There are many elements that go into building a brand. If you look at the most famous brands, you will see these elements are key in every single business:

- Company name
- Logo
- Slogan
- Message
- Tone
- Colors

You want to include all of these elements in your own business as well. Knowing how to incorporate these into your own brand will ensure that you are positioning yourself in a way that will allow you to generate maximum success in your company.

Company Name: You want to choose a company name for your business. This is a pivoting point for those who want to generate success in their business. Many will enter the business and go by the name of the company they are selling for. If you truly want to set yourself apart and give yourself the opportunity to generate massive success in your business, you will want to create your own business name. Think of it this way, many major retailers have a company name and then they sell products from other companies. If you build your company this way, you give yourself the opportunity to expand your business into other areas. While most network marketing companies will not let you cross-promote between various network marketing companies, you can still expand in other ways. One popular and the massively successful way that people grow their business is by starting out as a network marketer and then adding a consulting or coaching element to their business.

Logo: Every company has a logo. Investing in one for your business is a great way to set you apart from others and expand your business. Remember to pay attention to the rules in your company to ensure, however, that you are not breaking any rules around the branding structure of your business.

Slogan: Your slogan is important, this is something you want to use regularly so that people will think about your business right away when they hear your catchphrase or see your slogan. Your slogan should embody your brand's message in about 10 words or less. This is something that should be quick and easy to say, and it should be catchy. When people hear it, it should stick in their mind.

Message: Your message is essentially what we determined in the previous section of this chapter. Determining your exact message is extremely important. The best way to build a message for your brand is to pick one major message, and about three sub-messages to put underneath it. This could look something like this: "We aim to help people take control over their health. Our brand embodies drive, body confidence, and acceptance." When you have a message that has sub-messages underneath it, it gives more depth to your brand and allows you to have more to say without sounding as though you are repeating yourself. Everything you share for your brand should embody your brand message.

Tone: This is going to be how you feel when you are sharing your brand's message. Are you excited? Serious? Compassionate? Your tone allows you to share your message more effectively. It can be used to choose how you want your audience to feel when they hear your message, so take the time to really consider this. For example, if you want your audience to feel motivated to take control over their health, you will want to be energetic and compassionate. This tone will allow you to motivate them to take control and feel confident that you are not going to judge them for the reason why they have not taken control of it until now. Really think about what you want your audience to feel like about your unique brand, and use this to determine your tone.

Colors: The company you are marketing for already has a brand, so they likely already have colors chosen for their brand. You can choose to use these colors for your own brand, or you can choose your own colors if you prefer. Ideally, you want to have about three main colors that are a part of your brand. This will allow you to keep everything color-coded and fit nicely together. If you choose too many colors or don't commit to any specific color, you might find that your marketing doesn't look as appealing as it could. Having brand colors will help keep everything looking good.

Next-Level Branding Strategies

Having the basic elements of your brand together and using them to create your own business is important. However, there are many ways that you can go above and beyond with your branding to ensure that you really stand out from the crowd. The following techniques are proven strategies that can help your brand stand out and be noticeable among all of the other companies out there.

User Experience: The company you are working with is likely to already have an user experience established. However, that doesn't mean you can't emphasize that experience or create your own. For example, many network marketing companies work by having sellers host parties for clients. The party is the "user experience", as it gets the product in front of individuals and allows the attendees to test products before buying them.

You can create your own unique user experience, however, by expanding on this or even changing it altogether. You might want to create your own party games, design your own signature party experience, or even customize the party to the host's unique desires. Alternatively, you might want to change the experience entirely. Instead of hosting parties, you may prefer to generate an online group or "society" where you add people who are interested in learning more about your products. In that online society, they can gain access to recent information about the company, sales, and other niche-relevant information.

Just because you are marketing for a company that has already been established doesn't mean you can't customize it and build your own user experience. Get creative, think about how you want your business to look, and use this as an opportunity to generate your own business success!

Know Your Products: The company you are selling for likely emphasizes on one or two products from their line. These products may be the "signature" products or are simply the best-selling products for your business. Many marketers will only pay attention to these and will encourage everyone to purchase these products. You don't have to.

Instead of selling the exact same product every other marketer is selling, get to know your products intimately. Then, choose the ones you like most and use these as your own signature products. Doing this allows you to talk about a unique aspect of your business, establish your own angle, and talk about something that most others aren't talking about. It also gives you the opportunity to really know your product lineup so that you can set your customers up for the products that are going to work best for them.

Have Fun: Many people jump into a network marketing company and get very serious about their business. This is important, but it can also take away from the success of your business. People want to join you because you're having fun, not because you jump in and get more stressed out than you would be in a 9-to-5 job. When you jump into a ready-made company, it can be easy to get overwhelmed. The people who are already in the company may seem to have it together and have had time to figure out the entire company. Give yourself time, and have fun with it! Get to know the company a little more each day, and pick one aspect of the business to master each week. Just because the company is already well-established doesn't mean you need to be instantly established when you jump in. Take your time and get to know the company and learn how you can master it to generate your own success.

Remember, people want to join you because you are having fun and because the company you are working with is helping you generate that fun in your life. They want to see that you are living the life they want to be living and that your business is a pivotal part of that ability. This is what will draw them into you, make them listen, and have them interested in joining you.

You do not want to fake the happiness and fun because this will become exhausting. Your team will also pick up on this, and it will have a negative reflection throughout your entire team and business. Instead, take the time to build it up in a way that feels good to you, and make sure you are genuinely having fun with your experience. Learn, grow, and enjoy the process. Help others do the same. As your team builds, make sure you generate a culture in your team that is fun and exciting. This type of culture will help your entire team thrive, and will have others wanting to be a part of your team, because they want to have fun while making money, too!

It is unlikely that you would support a brand that didn't have a fun energy to it. If a brand is too serious, it can become dull. It can also become exhausting, and can even cause you to feel drained of energy. Instead of having a dull business that is exhausting and drains the energy from yourself and your team, establish one that is fun and enjoyable, and that everyone wants to be a part of. Make your work feel like a party! After all, that is why you wanted to join a network marketing company, right? To generate a large amount of money while having fun and enjoying your experience.

Branding your business is crucial. It is important that you take the time to establish a brand that is going to set yourself apart from other marketers in your company. The more you focus on your brand and build a strong brand and message, the easier it will be for you to attract new customers and team members. People will know *exactly* what you are about, and they will be able to see and feel your passion for your business. As a result, they will feel more compelled to join in on the fun and become a part of your team. Make sure you take the time to set up your brand before you even start marketing for your business.

Chapter 3: Lead Generation

Leads are people who show interest in your business and who could potentially become clients or team members in the future. Without leads, you will struggle to have success in your business. You want to make sure that you are generating leads on a regular basis, and there are many excellent ways that you can do this. In this chapter, we are going to explore how you can build your own automated lead-generating systems, and how you can use this to take your business to the next level.

The Importance of Leads

Having strong lead-generating structures in place will stop you from obsessively marketing to your friends and family. It allows you to expand your warm market so that you have more people to market to and prevents you from becoming the "tacky marketer" that many network marketers are known for.

When you take the time to establish strong, efficient lead-generating structures, you set yourself apart from the rest of the business. Instead of being known as the pushy sales person who won't leave people alone, you stand out as a professional who is building a real business.

If you don't take the time to generate new leads, you will run out of people to market to and your business will not thrive. Generating new leads is easy, and will give you the advantage when it comes to building a company that is going to have great success in the long run. It also keeps your friends and family from becoming annoyed with you and avoiding you so that they don't get blasted with sales pitches.

Personally Acquired Lead Generation

Personally acquired leads are any that you acquire through personal action. These are people who respond to your social media posts, who you talk to in public, or who you otherwise gain through sharing your message.

Personally acquired leads are an important part of your business. People who reach out to you through your messages and your sharing are considered leads who are interested in your business. This means they are more likely to be qualified leads, or leads who are more likely to convert into customers or team members.

You can gain personally acquired leads through sharing your personal story, talking about your business, and effectively branding yourself. This should be one of your primary business building activities, as leads become clients and clients are the backbone of your business. You want to talk about your business on a daily basis, and share it as frequently as you can. However, refrain from forcefully sharing it or overwhelming people with your message. You want to be consistent, but not pushy. If you overshare, tell too much, or shove it down people's throats, they are not going to want to do business with you because you overwhelm them with marketing. It is more effective to take your time, share one or two times online and one or two times offline per day, and interact with those who interact with you about the business. The slower you take it, the more success you are going to have in your business.

Automated Lead Generation

Automated lead generation is a strategy that many network marketers do not take advantage of in their business. Automated lead generation is acquired typically by having a landing page that allows you to grow your email list through what is known as an "opt-in". Many people don't realize that this is a completely viable and smart option for those in a network marketing business.

A great way to generate your own lead generation is to build an inexpensive landing page through a website that provides you with a click-and-build website template. There are many available, so find one that fits your budget and allows you to build an attractive landing page that you can send your leads to.

Once you have chosen your platform, you want to make a very basic one-page website that allows you to share a bit of information about a free offering you have created and encourage people to give you their email in exchange for the free offering. Because you are doing this, you will want to use an automated emailing system that can automatically respond to your signups with an email that contains access to your freebie.

Your freebie can be anything you want it to be. The following list will give you an idea of what types of freebies you can offer in exchange for emails.

- How-To PDF documents (i.e., "How to Get the Perfect Smoky Eye" or "How to Build a Custom Workout Routine")
- Pre-Recorded Webinars (i.e., "5 Ways to Improve Your Health Organically" or "3 Things You Can Do to Lead a Happier Life")

- Pre-Scheduled Webinars (the same as pre-recorded, but users save a spot and hop on the webinar live with you, which gives you the opportunity to host a live question and answer session)
- A free 30-minute consultation (where you can learn more about their unique needs and provide them with information and product recommendations to help them)
- A niche-relevant eBook you wrote
- A free product coupon to use if certain conditions are met (ensure you inquire with your company to see if this is an acceptable marketing strategy with your business)

Building a freebie takes very little time, and can be used to generate leads. Since the freebie is specific to your business, you know that the leads are qualified.

If you want to take it a step further, you can include what is known as a "tripwire". This means that your email would include a time-sensitive offer that encourages people to sign up or make a purchase right away.

Organizing and Converting Leads

Organizing your leads is important. That is why it is recommended that you encourage personally acquired leads to sign up for your freebie, as this gets them on your email list and keeps all of your leads in an easy-to-find place. You could also have your leads written down on a piece of paper and have their contact information available, but this means that you have to individually contact each lead. While this can add a nice personal touch to your business, it also means that you will likely waste a lot of time on unqualified leads, or leads who likely won't buy from you.

Once you have your leads organized into your email list, you can start converting them! You do this by sending out regular newsletters to your leads. These newsletters should contain information about your business, any offerings the company may have, and any unique offerings you are hosting. You can also include a button to take them to your website, and a button to help them join your business if they are interested.

When you are sending out the emails, make sure that you are stocking them up with plenty of useful information. The entire email should not be 100% sales. While the occasional email can be built this way, most should be built with valuable information that can benefit your clients. This will help them learn and stay interested in your business, without feeling as though they are constantly being blasted with sales and offerings in their inbox. In other words, it gives them a reason to continue opening your emails so that when they are ready to buy, they are more likely to open your email and find information about current promotions or offerings.

Staying Relevant

Having the same freebie available all the time will eventually lead to your freebie not converting the same it once did. One great idea is to have twelve different freebies. This might sound like a lot, but remember that freebies are only supposed to be small tidbits of information offered on an opt-in basis. It may take you a couple of days to establish your freebies, but once they are made you won't have to do it again.

The reason why you would want to have twelve freebies is because then you can promote a new one each month. This will give your leads several opportunities to gain access to information that would interest them and keeps your page and business fresh and relevant.

It is important that you take the time to build strong lead-generating structures in your business. Taking your time and putting together a strong freebie that helps you grow your email list will ensure that you don't waste hours upon hours later on trying to generate new leads as your warm market becomes overwhelmed. You turn your business into a truly professional establishment that is able to easily build a client base and grow sustainably, in a way that feels good to you and to your clients and team. People are more likely to follow a professional than they are to follow someone who uses tacky and desperate marketing strategies that leave their audience feeling exploited and annoyed. The first step in doing that is to build your audience, which can easily be done through having a strong lead-generation platform in place.

Chapter 4: Making Sales

Once you have lead generation fixtures in place, you can start focusing on making sales! Depending on your existing experience in sales, this part may or may not be easy for you. Some people step into the business and know exactly what they need to do, and others need practice. If you are not one of the "natural" sellers, fear not! You can certainly grow your skills and become a masterful seller using the techniques below.

Marketing Your Products

The first step in making sales is knowing how tao market your products. There are many ways to market products and services, both online and offline. When it comes to network marketing, a lot of the techniques that are still commonly discussed are quite outdated. While you may make sales from these techniques, it could take you much longer to actually make sales this way. Instead, you want to market your products in a way that is more relevant to the current marketing trends.

Since your lead-generation platform is based on email marketing, you should certainly take advantage of this method. Create a regular schedule to release email newsletters, and use this as an opportunity to market to your email audience. This is an important marketing strategy to take advantage of because these individuals have already proved that they are qualified leads. Since they were already interested in your business and your free offering, you can feel confident that they are going to be curious about what you have to share.

When you are building your emails, make sure that you are making them content-friendly. If your emails are purely based on marketing products and services, people will be less likely to continue opening them. Add value that is separate from sales and offerings. For example, if you are a part of a scented wax company, you can talk about which waxes can be melted together to create new and unique scents. Or, you may talk about how certain scents have been known to induce calmness, or relaxation, or otherwise. Providing information like this gives your readers a reason to continue opening your emails. You can also provide promotions, offerings, sales, your opportunity, and other call-to-actions in the emails, but you want to make sure that they aren't taking over the entire email. This keeps a nice happy balance and encourages readers to read through your email every time. This means that when a good sale is going on that they would be interested in, they have opened the email and they can see what is available for them.

Another way to access your market is through social media. One popular platform is Facebook. While your personal Facebook page is already populated, you should refrain from making this your primary platform. Share on a regular basis, but do not overwhelm your feed with posts about your business. This will lead to your friends and family not paying attention to you. Instead, share about it on a regular basis but maintain your regular feed content as well. A better way is to have a Facebook group where you talk about your products. This is a spot where you can add people who are interested in your products to your group and you can communicate with them there. You can let them know about current offerings and promotions, help them use your products, and learn other great information that is relevant to your company's niche. This is another great place to generate qualified leads!

Aside from Facebook, Instagram and Twitter are also great places for you to post about your products and offerings. These areas are not restricted to friends-only and they allow for you to have your posts seen by a much larger audience if you remember to hashtag them correctly.

When you are posting on these sites, refrain from taking pictures that look like a catalog, or from using stock pictures or pre-made sales pictures that are made available by your company. While they may be attractive and professional, they are not what your audience is looking for. Network marketing is based on peer-to-peer sales, and your peers want to see *you* as the star of the post. Share pictures of you using the products, receiving the products, or sharing the products with friends. You can even share first impression videos of you opening the welcome kit or your mail parcels, as this allows you to let people in on your excitement.

If you are interested in in-person marketing, there are many opportunities you have as well. In fact, you might be surprised to learn how big your audience actually is when it comes to offline marketing. And, you don't have to overwhelm your friends, cashiers, baristas, or other individuals for your marketing and sales efforts.

One great way to get in front of your audience is to set up a booth at a local market that is relevant to your niche. You can set up a booth with your products, get people physically trying them, and offer a market-only offering. Getting yourself in front of your audience in the flesh and sharing your products with them as they physically try them is a great way to make sales. You can also host a prize giveaway where you collect emails to grow your lead generation.

If you are talking to someone and you are able to naturally begin discussing your products and services, absolutely take advantage of the opportunity. However, instead of giving them your contact information, ask for theirs. Ask for their name as well as their email address or phone number so that you can contact them for more information about your business and the products and services you offer. This leaves the contact into your hands, rather than theirs. Sometimes people get home and forget about businesses they've heard about after a busy day. If you take the initiative, you are more likely to have effective contact with potential clients. A good way to do this is to ask for their email address, then email them with product information. You can also mention that you have a value-packed newsletter and you could add them if they were interested in learning more about upcoming promotions and sales. This helps populate your email list, organize your offline leads, and gives you an opportunity to market to your personally acquired leads.

Becoming a Confident Seller

Making sells starts with marketing, but it also comes with being a confident seller. There are many ways that you can increase your confidence and boost your successful seller's ratings. The following techniques and strategies will help you increase your confidence while also generating higher levels of sales and conversions.

Know Your Product: the best way to build up your confidence as a salesperson is to know what you are marketing. Get to know your products intimately. Take the time to research each product, the benefits and values of it, and what makes it so popular with the buyers. The more you know about your product, the more confident you are going to feel in sharing them with your buyers because you will know exactly why someone would want to buy it. Many people don't like listening to sales people who don't know their own product, and many salespeople don't feel confident in selling a product that they don't know.

Know Your Client: in addition to knowing your product, take the time to get to know each individual client. Every client is going to have unique interests and needs, which you can learn about through your conversation with them. When you take the time to get to know what you are actually looking for, you make it possible for you to recommend the products that would truly benefit them. This shows that you care about your client and their happiness, and that you want them to have a positive experience with your business. When customers feel cared about in this way, they are more likely to become repeat customers. If they truly fall in love with the business, they may even choose to join your team.

Practice Talking About It, often: just because you aren't selling doesn't mean you can't be talking about your products! This is a great marketing strategy, and it gives you the opportunity to get to gain confidence in selling your products. Talk about your products whenever you naturally can. Good platforms to practice this include your social media platforms, your email newsletters, and in general conversation whenever the topic comes up.

Get Clients on The Phone: people are much less likely to make a purchase if they haven't personally connected with you. While direct messaging is a good opportunity to start a conversation, you should encourage the conversation to move to the phone or a video conference-style chat every single time. When you can get your voice, or better yet your face, in front of someone, you can better share your excitement about the product. People are more likely to talk to you when you get them on the phone than they are if you simply stick to direct messaging. The experience is more intimate and personal, and it has a better conversion rate.

Listen to Testimonials: take the time to interact with your existing customers, or existing customers of the company, to learn why people are so passionate about the products they are using. Understand what customers are attracted to, and what makes them want to continue using your products. If they did not have a particularly positive experience, learn why so that you can make it better in the future for them and other customers. This is the best way to really get an intimate understanding of what your clients are generally looking for, and therefore what you want to emphasize when you are selling your products.

Lead by Example: if you aren't using your products, you will have a much harder time converting clients. Make a point to try each product at least once so that you can understand what you are selling. Take the time to really get to know the product, and find out who it is best for. If you don't want to continue using the entire product, turn it into a demo product that you can use to try with your friends and family or people at markets who are interested in testing the products. This allows you to show first-hand that you love your products and are passionate about them. It also helps you show your excitement to your audience.

Go at the Pace of Your Client: take your time with your client. Don't jump immediately into a pitch before they've even had time to ask questions about your company and product. Give them a chance to ask questions, and take the time to answer them. While you want to lead the conversation towards a sale, you don't want to jump straight into it before your client is ready. Make sure you look for cues that they are interested in knowing more and then take those cues to lead the conversation forward.

If Not Today, Set Yourself Up for Tomorrow: don't write off a potential sale just because it didn't go through today. If you are taking the time to genuinely connect with people and talk to them about your business and your products, you are planting seeds for the future. Just because they don't buy right away doesn't mean they won't buy ever. And even if they won't buy ever, if you leave a good impression they will be more likely to refer people to you as opposed to others in the business who may begin to treat them differently after they decide not to purchase your products. Remember, you want your business to remain sustainable, and planting seeds today is a great way to grow your potential for tomorrow.

Selling your products is a necessary part of staying in business. By learning to become a confident seller and mastering your own products, you will find selling to be an effortless reality of your business. In fact, when you become used to it, it can even become fun! The best way to truly become successful and confident with selling for your business is by practicing. Get used to talking to the client, talking about your products, and finding products that perfectly match your clients. The better you get with each of these three elements, the easier selling will become for you. Even if you aren't currently experienced with the art of sales, you will be able to master it using these techniques.

Chapter 5: Building a Team

One of the major parts of being a network marketer is building a team. Building a team gives you the opportunity to uplevel your business and make even more money. It also further positions you as a master in your industry. People like to look up to the people who are leading the businesses, which means that more people are going to be attracted to your team. Building a team gives you the opportunity to generate passive income, and can even give you the opportunity to stop selling and just nurture your team as it continues to grow over time.

There are many techniques presently floating around about how you can and should build your team, but a large amount of it is completely false. If you follow some of the strategies that are being shared among network marketers, not only will your team fail, but you will become quickly burnt out with your efforts. In this chapter, we are going to discuss effective and professional strategies to build your network marketing team and help you expand your business.

The Importance of Your Team

Your team is a vital part of your business. As previously mentioned, having a strong team in the network marketing industry means that you can step into even more of a leadership role and that you no longer have to sell if you don't want to. While you will want to retain your present customer base, most of your income will come from having a strong team.

Not only does your growing team give you a passive income potential, but it also changes the shape of your business. In addition to selling great products and services, you also get to lead others towards changing their lives and the lives of their own teams. Additionally, you establish a team which is a great experience in itself. Your team is a lot like your colleagues and coworkers, only everyone wants to be there. The energy of your team can be exhilarating, and can also lead to many new friendships being built within' business and within' life itself.

Your team is necessary. If you want to expand your business and have great success in the network marketing industry, you need to start building a team. There are many ways that you can do this, but the following strategies will ensure that you do it effectively, efficiently, and that you are building a strong team in the process. Regardless of what anyone else may tell you, *these* are the proven strategies that are going to take you to the top.

Start Early

The first thing you must do when you are building your business is start early. The earlier you assume a leadership role, the sooner you are going to start building a team. People want to join a business if they see that they are joining under a strong leader who can genuinely help them in the process of building success. To put it simply, people will not follow a leader.

You want to start being a leader before you even have a team. In other words, from the day you establish your brand and launch your business, you want to assume a leadership role. There are many ways that you can start taking on this leadership role, well before you even become a leader. Many people will tell you that you should do this by jamming your authority in the faces of your potential downline. The opposite is actually true. A leader that others want to follow is someone who is passionate, knowledgeable, and strong. People want a leader who clearly assumes authority, is confident in their authority, and who appear to know exactly what it takes to lead them to success.

If you are pushy, attempting to force your authority, or are otherwise trying to encourage people to see you as a leader, there is a good chance that you will come off as desperate. Leaders are confident, and that means they don't have to assert their authority because it is assumed based on their actions.

Of the actions you can take to assume a leadership position, one of the most important is to have a huge vision and never lose it. Take the time to share it with your audience, and regularly remind them of your vision. Try your best to accentuate different parts of the vision so that you are not continually repeating yourself, and so that your story stays fresh and relevant to your audience. You want them to see your passion without feeling as though you are constantly saying the exact same thing. Show them what your vision looks like, share parts of your vision as they come to life, and keep them informed without being repetitive or pushy.

Another way is to set a daily routine that you are committed to. Leaders are effective and efficient, and they spend their time doing money-building activities that are positive for their business. If you start doing this right from the get go, people are going to see you as a leader who is committed to your own success. If you can prove that you are committed to your own success, people will feel more confident in your commitment to their success as well.

Before you even establish a team, you should also establish a basic training module for them to complete. This can be a free PDF file or video that you send to them when they sign up for your team. This document should provide them with information to help them get started in their own business, as well as to give them anything they need to know about generating success. You can also include information about who they can turn to for help in various areas.

Lastly, you want to think like a leader. A leader is always looking out for the success of their team. Start doing this right away with your clients, so that they see how dedicated you are to the success of everyone involved with your business. When your clients see your dedication and your commitment to your team, they will be more likely to convert into team members because they feel confident that you can lead them towards success.

This is a vital step that many network marketers fail to appreciate. Knowing how to lead a team before you even have a team means that you will be an even stronger leader when your team starts growing. When you already have this experience and already have resources in place for your team, it gives them a great launching pad to help them generate massive success in their own business. This means that people will be much more likely to join your team because they feel that they have all of the knowledge, support, and resources required to generate success quickly.

Pick the Right People

When it comes to building your team, make sure you take the time to pick the right people. Many network marketers emphasize on the numbers more than they do the quality of their team members. This is because you often get bonuses or compensation for every member that signs up underneath you. However, if you are pushing people to join who are not actually qualified for or truly interested in the opportunity, you are going to experience failure in your team.

A better idea is to be really intentional about what types of people you are aiming to add to your team. They should be people who genuinely want to be a part of it, and who are likely to generate massive success because they are committed to the process. While you don't have to say no to someone who is adamant about being on your team whether you believe they will commit or not, you do want to make sure that you aren't pursuing or putting pressure on the wrong people who truly won't be an asset to your team.

Just as with any business, you want to focus on quality over quantity when it comes to your team. Remember, each quality member that you add will add several members under them. However, if you are adding people who do not genuinely care about the opportunity and who are not committed to success, then you are going to end up having to replace many members on your team as your team crumbles around you.

Nurture Your Team

As your team grows, you want to continue to nurture them. There are many ways that successful network marketing leaders are generating success on their team through nurturing their team members. You can do this on your own team using their strategies for success. These strategies are outlined below.

Team-Specific Groups: having team-specific groups created on social media is a great way to unite your team and create a team-like setting. In the past, it was difficult to communicate with members of your team if they did not live near you. Now, you can communicate with your team all over the globe. Having a team-only group available for members gives them a place to share their experiences, teach each other lessons, and encourage each other to grow in the business. It also gives you and your team members a great marketing strategy when it comes to signing new sellers. People *love* joining a team-like setting where a group of people are dedicated to helping them succeed. The team is often one of the most attractive parts of the opportunity, so making sure that your team is powerful, positive, and supportive will help ensure that you have great success in your business.

Live Meet Ups: as you make more and more money in your business, make an honest attempt to host live meet ups in areas where you have many team members. This gives each member an opportunity to come together for a team-building experience where they can all get to know one another, build relationships, and support each other in their journeys. While most companies will host one large company-wide meeting per year, you can take the initiative and host ones specific for your own team. This helps establish you as a strong and caring leader and boosts the morale and community in your business.

Video Conferences: similar to live meet ups, video conferences are an excellent opportunity for your team to come together and build relationships while also boosting morale. You can host a conference to share tips, information, and upcoming promotions or offers. You can also have members on your team ask questions and get answers, share their own advice or information, and contribute to the knowledge and success of the team. You can, and should, host regular video conferences for your team.

1:1 Support with New Team Members: building your team can be even easier if you have exclusive 1:1 support for new members that join your team. You can offer this support yourself, or you can teach other members on your team to do the same for new members. The bigger your team grows, the more help you will need in this department. Aim to become not only a master at selling and building your own business but a master at helping others do the same. If you can coach others to build success in their business from the get go, you will have a much higher success rate on your team overall.

Updated Training Workbooks: you want to take the time to continually update the trainings you make for your team. Just like you had training made at the beginning for your brand new team, continue to update and create training over time. A great idea is to do several training sessions for various aspects of the business. For example, you might have training dedicated to helping new team members succeed, marketing and sales strategies, building a team, and more. Make sure these remain updated, and that they are made available to your team members so they can access the training and expand their successful businesses!

Live Video Training: in addition to doing live video conferences, you should offer live video training. This will give you the opportunity to teach your team how to succeed in real-time. In fact, you may prefer to do this as an alternative to the evergreen training that was recommended in the previous section. If you want, you can schedule regular training sessions that you complete live for all new team members and existing team members. That way, they can jump on live and get help in real-time, as well as ask questions and get answers right away. You should do regular live training for your team to help them succeed in their business.

Team Building Activities: hosting regular team-building activities is a great way to create success for your team. You can host a variety of different activities with the intention of building your team morale and create and nurture relationships on your team. You can do online or offline activities.

Simply get creative, and go! Some great ideas include: encouraging new members to do a live video and introduce themselves and the reason why they have joined your business, a "product knowledge" scavenger hunt to encourage team members to learn more about products and potentially win a prize at the end, team chats, and more.

Nurturing your team is a necessary part of having a successful team. You don't want to simply sign people up under you, you want to support them in their success. Remember, the more success your team creates, the more success you are going to experience overall. If you want to rise to the top of your network marketing business, you need to be dedicated to your team and help them establish success in their lives.

Encourage Growth

In addition to growing your own team, you want to encourage your team to grow their own teams. The bigger each of their teams grows, the bigger your own team grows. This is an important part of building your business. You don't want to be the only one recruiting new sellers. You want to have everyone dedicated to the success of the entire team. There are many ways that you can encourage your team to generate growth.

One great way to encourage growth is to have your team members help out with team training and growth. Encourage your team members to host their own training videos, or to go live with you and discuss success-building tips and habits for your business. The more you welcome your team members to help you in building your team, the more confident they are going to feel in building their own. This is a great hands-on way to train the go-getters on your team how to build their own team and success.

Another great way is to host "challenges", where you encourage your team to add more members each month or quarter and reward them with a giveaway or some other type of reward for succeeding in the challenge. Remember, however, to encourage your team to add genuine members and not simply people who will help them reach their count.

You can also help your team grow by providing your special free training and free resources to the team members that your personally recruited members add to the business. Give them the exclusive opportunity to gain access to your training sessions so that they feel special for getting access to the training that is responsible for building a highly successful team already.

Remember, growing your team is not entirely up to you. If you are adding genuine and effective team members, you are going to have success in creating a team of people that are dedicated to growing their own teams. This means that with a little help, they will be building their own teams and you will all grow.

Remain a Leader

One thing you must remain dedicated to is being a leader for your team. If you do not remain a leader, your team will crumble beneath you. You want to make sure that you remain dedicated to being a leader to the team that you work so hard to build. The best way is to continue nurturing your team and encouraging the growth within' your team. You can do this through regular live training sessions, live video conferences, in-person meetups, and more.

People don't want to see you reach your desired success and then fade away as you ride by on the passive income you have built. This will show them that you are not honest and that you are not truly dedicated. They want to see that you remain dedicated regardless of how much success you generate. Make sure you take the time to continue being the leader and leading your team, no matter how big it gets or how much your income grows.

Your team is the lifeline of your business, much in the same way that your clients are. When you are building your business, you need to take the time and care to build your team. You don't only want to focus on gathering clients because then you must continue gathering more and more in order to stay successful. Instead, you want to build a team so that you can offload some of the linear work and build a passive income as well. The more you are dedicated to your success overall, the larger your business will grow and the more success you will experience.

Chapter 6: Growing Your Business

The process of growing your business is more simple than you might think. You may look at people in the network marketing industry who have massive teams and think that as their workload grows they become more weighted down in increased responsibilities. The opposite is actually true. In fact, building your network marketing business is easier than it looks.

The biggest thing you should know is that you have to repeat your business building processes over, and over again. That is: you want to be a leader, build your team, and repeat. The more you assume a leadership role, the larger your team will grow. Fulfilling the leadership responsibilities and roles provided in the previous chapter will help you have major success in your business.

In addition, however, there are many ways that you can increase your own success so that you can increase the success of your team and therefore grow your business even larger. The more you focus on growth in your business, the larger your team will grow and the more success you will all experience together. The following information will provide you with the strategies you need to grow your business, in addition to everything you have already learned in this book.

Continually Practice Being a Better Leader

When you are building your business, you want to continually practice being a better leader. Always focus on your leadership abilities, and look for opportunities to expand your success as a leader. You should remain dedicated to your own success, as well as the success of others. Take the time to acquire feedback from your team, complete leadership-oriented training seminars, and classes, and continue studying what successful leaders are doing in business. Remember, you can take leadership advice from people beyond the network marketing world. A powerful leader is a powerful leader, and they all have excellent advice and information for you to adapt for your own business. The more time you invest in becoming a powerful leader, the greater your business is going to grow.

Take Part in the Existing Team as Well

If you built your business properly, you likely have a great team above you already. Your upline likely has a great team who are supportive and models many of the qualities that you want your own team to have. In the beginning, you can use this as an opportunity to provide massive support for your new recruits. You can add your new recruits to your own business group, as well as to any groups hosted by your upline. Encourage them to become really active in your group, but remind them that your upline has a strong existing support team available as well.

Additionally, take part in the team that exists above you. Take the time to bond with other leaders, and other members who are at the same level as you are. This will give you the opportunity to expand your own team's resources, gain information about how you can succeed as a leader, and otherwise encourage the success of your business.

It is likely that your upline has spent a long time generating success in their own business, so taking advantage of the support and culture that they have already built. This is a great way to network for your business and increase your ability to expand the success of your own team.

Take Advantage of New Marketing Opportunities

Over time, new marketing opportunities are rapidly becoming available. In the past, parties, word of mouth, and business cards were major marketing opportunities for people in network marketing companies. Nowadays, social media is where the bulk of the business is done. Over time, the strategies that are used to generate successful marketing campaigns evolve. Since you want to maintain a relevant and sustainable business, you want to take advantage of these new marketing opportunities as they arise.

While you don't need to spend every day invested in new marketing strategies, you should certainly revisit your marketing techniques every two to three months. This will allow you to notice the evolving trends in the online marketplace and get a good idea of what is sticking and what was a passing fad. The ones that stick are the ones that you want to invest in when it comes to your own business.

You can also take the time to really understand these strategies and create new training videos or hosting training seminars for your team. Helping them understand what new marketing strategies are presently working will ensure that they are using relevant and effective strategies that will help them grow their business more successfully.

Network, Network, Network!

You are running a network marketing company, after all! Networking is a major part of building your success in this business. You want to take the time to really learn how you can build genuine relationships with other people in your business and attract new people in. Learn what it takes to generate powerful relationships with your customers, your potentials, your team members, and anyone else associated with your business.

Networking gives you the opportunity to gain new ideas, share your business opportunity, and get your product in front of more people. The more you focus on networking, the more success you will have in your business. People are attracted to a charismatic leader who is social and who can make everyone feel comfortable and welcomed into the business. Whether you are already a natural at this or you need to build your networking skills, it is worth noting.

If you are unsure as to where you can start, a good idea is to join niche-specific groups and business-oriented groups with many like-minded people. You can communicate with other business owners and others who are passionate in your niche and start building relationships. This can be done through online groups, or through offline groups. Either way, be very intentional about where you commit your time and devote your time and attention to these areas. For example, if you join an online group make sure that you spend a few minutes each day communicating with the members inside of the group. This will ensure that they know who you are, and can spark a curiosity in them to learn more about what you do and what your business is all about.

Networking is the backbone of your business, so you need to practice with it. You should also teach your team to do the same. The more successful you are with networking, the more success you are going to have overall.

Make a Schedule and Stick to It

Having a business schedule can be very helpful when it comes to running your own business, especially one with a larger team. It can be easy to get overwhelmed with work or become uncertain about where you want to devote your time to each day. By making a schedule, you can ensure that you know what to do each day. Make your schedule realistic and easy to accomplish so that you are able to stay on top of it each day. Keep your tasks intentional, and make sure you focus on money-building and team-building tasks that are going to have a large impact on your business.

Some things you might want to include on your schedule include:

- Networking
- Team-building activities
- Training and live conference calls
- Live events
- New offers and opportunities
- New free offerings (unique to your personal business)

Every successful business runs on a schedule. You should also include your "opening" hours so that you know when your working hours are, and when they aren't. This means that you can focus on business-building activities during working hours and that you disconnect and focus on your personal life when it is not business hours.

Stay Focused on Morale

The morale of your brand and your team is important. The morale you boost on your team will have a heavy influence on your success in the business overall. Make sure that you are regularly promoting a positive, energetic, and success-oriented morale in your team. If you notice that your morale is falling low, that certain team members aren't getting along, or that you aren't having the type of impact you want to have, it is time to take action and build success in your business.

As the leader, it is your job to take control of the morale being generated by the business and really make sure that everyone is feeling excited and energetic about their own businesses. The more you can encourage people to stay positive and focused, the more success you will have in your business overall.

Build Leaders

When you are building your business, focus on building leaders as well. Take notice of the go-getter style members on your team and really encourage them to take a leadership role. These are the members who are most likely to be able to generate their own successful teams, and they are the ones who are going to be dedicated to the success of everyone overall.

Some ways you can build your leaders include through inviting them to host live training events for your team, giving them unique and personalized 1:1 training to help them excel as leaders, and helping them build their own teams.

Unlike the other members who you are coaching to succeed as business owners, you want to coach these members to become business executives. These are the members that are more likely to grow massive teams, just as you are. The more successful they are at growing these teams, the more successful you will be. This is an important part of the business.

Nurture Your Personal Life

One important way to remain successful in business is to maintain your personal life. Many people join network marketing companies because it affords them the freedom to be their own bosses and thus, to take the time in their day to enjoy it in any way that they like. People don't want to see that you are working harder in your network marketing business than you ever did at your regular job because then they are not going to be attracted to the network marketing lifestyle.

Instead, they want to see that you are having fun and living your life. They want to see that you are enjoying the freedom that they are seeking to experience in their own lives. Ultimately, they want to see you sharing the adventures you go on, the hours you spend relaxing, and the way you enjoy your time with family and friends. People are nosy, and they want to see directly into your life. They want to know that you are modeling the life they want to live because then they know that you will know exactly how to help them do the same. They want a leader who is actively leading the life they desire to have.

Keep It Simple

Many people might feel convinced that they have to go to extensive lengths to establish a business model that will help them succeed. They feel as though they have to fulfill complex strategies and roles in order to have a network marketing company that will be effective and bring in both passive and linear income. The reality is, this is not true. In fact, the aim is to keep it simple. The simpler your business structures are, the more success you will be able to generate with them.

Remember: you want to be a leader, sell products, and grow your team. That is all. You want to take the time to invest in strategies that are going to help you succeed with these efforts and strategies. The more focused you are on these strategies, the more success you are going to have. You do not need to waste your time investing in complex and advanced strategies that are unlikely to acquire larger results than the easier strategies. These types of techniques will simply generate success and leave you feeling burnt out and confused about where to go in your business.

In addition, complex and advanced strategies are difficult to replicate. If your team can't easily apply the strategies in their own business, they are too difficult. You want to keep everything as simple as possible and give your team the best opportunity to succeed. This will increase your own success, as well as the success of everyone you are seeking to assist with your business.

Stay Motivated

As with any business, there are going to be periods in your network marketing company where things are "down" or not as productive as normal. In fact, many people experience a "down" period right out the gate. While you are building your structures, spreading your message, and becoming known for your business, it can be slow rolling. Some people come out of the gate hot, but not everyone does. In fact, most people find that it takes six to twelve months for them to add their first team member. This is not unusual, and it is not the reason for you to quit.

The more dedicated you remain and the more consistent you are at building your systems and structures and creating a successful business, the more sustainable your business will be. You always want to pay attention to the "tomorrow" in your business. Sometimes, the "today" may not look bright, and that is okay. Every business has ups and downs, and every business takes time to grow. The more you remain consistent and focused on your growth and success, the more you and your team will experience. Stay dedicated, and do what you have to in order to stay motivated.

Growing your business is necessary if you want to have a sustainable and successful business. It can take time, as well as dedication, but the more you stay focused the greater your business will grow. There are many ways that you can build your business, but ultimately you want to stay focused on the business-building activities that will help you grow your sales numbers and expand your team. These are the two areas of your business that will help you generate income, so they are where you want to stay focused during all of your business activities.

Conclusion

Thank you for reading *Network Marketing: The Complete Guide to Create a Profitable Network Marketing Business Using Online Strategies and Techniques (Learn Proven Online and Social Media Techniques That Will Propel Your Business to the Next Level).*

I hope that you were able to learn all about how you can build a successful network marketing business. From choosing your company and establishing your brand to growing your sales and building a team, there are many activities that go into building your business successfully. It is important that you understand these activities and their importance so that you can have success in building your own network marketing business.

Remember, the industry is presently filled with a significant amount of advice that is ineffective and that may actually take your business in the opposite direction from where you want to go. It is important that you take the time to choose structures that are effective and that are going to help you create next-level success as quickly as possible. The sooner you ditch these ineffective strategies and take advantage of successful and proven strategies, the sooner you are going to experience massive success in your business.

The next step in creating success in your business is to start at the beginning of this book. If you have not already chosen your company or established a recognizable brand, then it is time to do so. You want to take the time to build this solid foundation so that your entire business can thrive with these basic structures in place. Having your brand easily identifiable and recognizable means that you will look even more professional in the eyes of your clients and team members, which is important if you want to generate next-level success in your business.

Once you have established your branding, you can go ahead and start practicing selling and building a team. Then, simply continue building your sales and nurturing your team. Over time, these strategies will help you grow beyond your wildest dreams. You will be able to take your business to the next level, and then the next level, and eventually the top level.

Lastly, if you enjoyed this book, I ask that you please take the time to review it on Amazon Kindle. Your honest feedback would be greatly appreciated

Thank you, and best of luck in your network marketing business!